SCIENCE MUSEUM

TALKING MACHI

V K Chew

Students and F

LONDON HER MAJESTY'S STATIONERY OFFICE

Foreword

The preparation of a second edition of this booklet
has provided an opportunity of eliminating many
of the errors that were inevitable in the pioneering
first edition. If this aim has been achieved it is due
almost entirely to the generosity of expert readers who
responded so promptly to requests for suggested
corrections. Thanks are due in particular to Mr
Allen Koenigsberg, Mr Raymond Wile, Mr Frank
Andrews and Mr Leonard Petts, who contributed so
much that they ought really to be regarded as
co-authors.

Thanks are due also to the editors and contributors
of those remarkable examples of voluntary effort the
Antique Phonograph Monthly the *Hillandale News*
and the *Talking Machine Review International.* Study
of these periodicals has led, not only to the correction
of error, but also to the addition of some material to
the text, where this could be done without trans-
gressing the deliberately imposed restrictions on the
scope of the booklet.

A number of illustrations have been added; a few
have been eliminated and an index has been provided.

© *Crown copyright 1981*
First published 1967
Second edition 1981
ISBN 0 11 290329 0

Contents

Notes

The prices of instruments and records quoted in this booklet are on the old £ s d system for which 1s = 5p and 2·4d = 1p.

The metrical equivalents of the dimensions of cylinders and discs quoted are:

inches	mm
1	25·4
3	76
4	102
4½	114
5	127
6	152
7	178
8¾	222
10	254
10½	267
12	305
14	356
16	406
20	508

The abbreviation for a dimension expressed in inches is ″ (eg 6″)

Introduction

When Edison invented a means of recording sound and reproducing it at will he became the founder of an industry which was recently called, not without some justification, the 'industry of human happiness'. The pioneers of this industry called the instruments they devised phonographs, graphophones and gramophones; the only name covering them all that was generally accepted was 'talking machine'. If we employ this term to mean an instrument that reproduced sound from a record without the aid of electronic amplification, then we see in the talking machine an instrument of the past. It was born in 1877 and it was dead, in the sense that no further development took place, by 1939. Young people today see talking machines only in museums where they survive not, we hope, as dusty relics with an appeal based only on their quaintness, but as the tangible evidence of the birth and growth of a new human activity in which scientists, engineers, artists, financiers and merchants co-operated or competed, found affluence, subsistence or ruin in an attempt to satisfy an almost universal demand for musical entertainment by a population enjoying, for the first time, the leisure to appreciate it.

This booklet makes no claim to be even a sketch of the history which this intensely interesting human activity deserves. It is concerned only with the talking machine itself and makes only passing references to the recording process, to the music recorded and to the artists concerned. After following the story of the instrument in its country of origin until 1902, it deals only with the European activities of the American talking machine companies. It mentions developments in Germany and, to a lesser extent, in France, only in so far as it is necessary to explain their impact on the British market. It closes in 1914, a date which, as far as the talking machine is concerned, is somewhat arbitrary. But despite these limitations it is hoped that the booklet will supplement any pleasure that visitors may gain from inspecting the talking machines in the Science Museum collection, and will encourage them to read the more extensive histories listed in the Appendix.

The first talking machine was constructed by Thomas Alva Edison (1847–1931) late in 1877. Human speech had been recorded and reproduced for the first time in July of the same year. On this occasion, according to Edison's associate Charles Batchelor, "Mr Edison had a telephone diaphragm mounted in a mouth-piece of rubber in his hand, and he was sounding notes in front of it and feeling the vibration of the centre of the diaphragm with his finger. After amusing himself with this for some time, he turned round to me and he said: 'Batch, if we had a point on this, we could make a record on some material which we could afterwards pull under the point and it would give us the speech back'." The experiment was tried, using a waxed strip of paper as the recording medium, and it was successful.

Edison had thus constructed a very crude talking machine but this aspect of the invention was not uppermost in his mind; he regarded it as a device that could have some application in telephony. It might, for example, provide a reproducible record of a telephone message, or a means whereby a person without a telephone could record a message for subsequent transmission from a central office. He therefore continued to work on it with such ends in view. It is not known what diverted him from this to the construction of the phonograph but in spite of some improbabilities and some definite inaccuracies in his telling of the tale there may be a grain of truth in an assertion by E Johnson, another associate of Edison, that when in early November he was lecturing on Edison's recent inventions, he mentioned the tele-

Thomas A Edison

1 T A Edison

phone relay and the enthusiastic reaction by his audience to the news that the human voice could be recorded and reproduced convinced him, and through him Edison, that this was the significant aspect of the invention and not any possible application to telephony. Whatever the stimulus, a letter by Johnson in an issue of the *Scientific American* which was dated 17 November, but which appeared on the 6th, makes it clear that Edison was engaged on improving the paper strip phonograph and the result of his work was the tinfoil phonograph, which was sketched in his notebook on 29 November, successfully constructed by his mechanic, John Kruesi, modified and completed to his satisfaction on 6 December and demonstrated in the office of the editor of the *Scientific American* on the following day. A strong tradition encourages us to believe that the first words recorded and reproduced by Kruesi's original model were 'Mary had a little lamb'.

The instrument thus produced consisted of a brass drum, about four inches in diameter, on the circumference of which was incised a helical groove with a

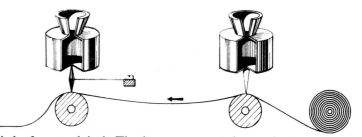

2 Sketch of Edison's proposed telephone repeater, 1877

pitch of one tenth inch. The drum was mounted on an axle so threaded and supported that one rotation of the handle at the end moved the drum laterally through one tenth inch. On one side of the drum was the recorder consisting of a mouthpiece terminating in a diaphragm having at its centre a stylus in contact with the tinfoil, the pressure of this contact being variable by means of a lateral adjustment of the recorder. On the other side of the drum was the reproducer with the same general construction as the recorder, but having a more flexible diaphragm. To record, the speaker adjusted the position of the drum until the stylus of the recorder was near one end of it and above the groove and then spoke into the mouthpiece while

3 Replica of Edison's tinfoil phonograph, 1877

3

4 Charles Cros

duced sounds he was not the first to conceive that such a process was possible and to suggest a means of achieving it. This was done by the Frenchman Charles Cros (1842–1888) who in his brief life of 46 years studied philology, taught chemistry, practised medicine, invented a process of colour photography, devised a radiometer and a process of facsimile telegraphy, wrote poems that earned the praise of Verlaine and became a leader of the Bohemian society of Paris, which he entertained by his revival of the art of the comic monologue. His proposals for a phonograph first became known to the public through an article in *La Semaine du Clergé* of 10 October 1877 but they had been deposited in a sealed packet with the Academy of Sciences on 30 April 1877 and this packet was opened at his request on 3 December 1877.

Cros proposed to attach a stylus to a diaphragm and to allow the end of the stylus to touch the smoke-blackened surface of a disc of transparent material which was subject to a double motion of rotation and linear translation. If the diaphragm were at rest the stylus would trace out a simple spiral on the disc; if it were vibrating, the result would be an undulating spiral. This spiral was to be transformed by well-known photographic processes into a similar spiral, engraved or in relief, on a disc of hard material such as tempered steel. This disc was to be subject to the appropriate motion of rotation and translation, and to reproduce the sound by vibrating a diaphragm by means of a stylus constrained by a spring to ride in or on the recorded spiral. Cros patented his invention in May 1878 but he failed to make a working model of this device and, more significantly, he failed in his attempt to secure for it the interest of Breguet, of the illustrious family firm of instrument makers. But the idea was brilliant; it anticipated Edison, and there are some whose definition of the term 'inventor' allows them to regard Cros rather than Edison as the inventor of the talking machine.

rotating the handle as uniformly as possible. The process produced indentations in the tinfoil corresponding to the sound vibrations of the speech. To reproduce, the recorder was withdrawn and the drum counter-rotated until the reproducer stylus could be set in contact with the beginning of the indented groove. The handle was again rotated and the diaphragm of the reproducer, vibrating in accordance with the indentions of the tinfoil, gave forth a distorted reproduction of the original speech.

Although Edison was undoubtedly the first man to produce an instrument that recorded and repro-

The original tinfoil phonograph was seen, possibly before it was demonstrated to the American public, by Henry Edmunds, a British engineer then engaged on a study tour in the USA. On his return to England he wrote to *The Times* about it and the British public learnt of the invention from an article in that newspaper published on 17 January 1878. Readers of the *English Mechanic* had already heard about it through a letter from Charles Batchelor dated 9 December and published on 4 January. Mr W H Preece (later Sir William Preece and Engineer-in-Chief and Electrician of the General Post Office) immediately arranged for a tinfoil phonograph to be constructed by his colleague A Stroh under the guidance of Edmunds and this instrument was demonstrated to an audience at the Royal Institution on 1 February, at the end of a lecture on the telephone. For a lecture to the Society of Telegraph Engineers on 27 February Preece had three instruments at his disposal. The first was a copy of the original Edison instrument, made by W Pidgeon, an amateur. The second was an improved model sent by Edison in the hand of his foreign patent lawyer Mr Puskas. This model was provided with a heavy flywheel to secure greater uniformity of rotation, and it had only a single diaphragm and stylus, used both for recording and reproduction. The third, constructed by Stroh, also employed a single diaphragm, but the drum was driven by a clockwork motor operated by a falling weight, the speed being governed by means of a fan mechanism. This latter development is significant of the fact that the phonograph was hailed in England

5 W H Preece demonstrating the tinfoil phonograph, 1878

5

6 Edison tinfoil phonograph; improved model with flywheel

right
7 Tinfoil phonograph with gravity motor, 1878

and in Europe generally as a scientific instrument rather than a scientific toy. The London Stereoscopic Company was licensed to exploit the Edison patent in Great Britain and an instrument dealer's catalogue of 1886 lists three models supplied by this firm; the first, hand-cranked and without flywheel, at £5, the second with a flywheel at £10 10s 0d and the third, driven by a falling weight, at £25.

One scientific problem to which it was hoped that the phonograph would provide a solution was that of the nature of vowel sounds. Since Helmholtz had discussed the matter in *Sensations of Tone* (1st Edition 1863) two rival theories had been advocated and, as Lord Rayleigh pointed out in 1894, '. . . Edison's beautiful invention of the phonograph stimulated a new inquiry on this subject by apparently affording easy means of making an *experimentum crucis*'. The method proposed was to record a vowel sound, to reproduce it at different speeds and to see whether the character as well as the pitch of the sound depended on the speed of reproduction. The experiments were inconclusive but, taken in conjunction with the fact that the phonograph had been listed by W Stone in

1881 as one of the devices whereby the frequency of a musical note could be determined, they gave the instrument an academic dignity which Edison could hardly have expected.

6

The respect of the British public for the great inventor was stimulated by the fact that for many years they were able to inspect the original phonograph itself. In 1880 an official of the Patent Office Museum, while visiting the USA, called on Edison and secured this historic instrument from him. A few years later it made a brief cross-Channel excursion to join Edison's stand at the Paris Exhibition of 1889.

8 Edison's stand at the Paris Exhibition, 1889

With other objects in the Patent Office Museum it ultimately became part of the Science Museum collection and remained there until 1928, when it was returned to the USA on Edison's request and formally handed back to him by a representative of the British Government at a ceremony during which the inventor was presented with the Congressional Medal.

The obviously advantageous step of fitting a spring motor to the phonograph proved to be unexpectedly difficult. J E Greenhill, a London inventor and lecturer on scientific matters, worked on this task for a number of years, starting in the tinfoil era. It was not until 1893, when the tinfoil phonograph was a thing of the past, that Greenhill had the satisfaction of seeing a spring motor of his design, manufactured by William Fitch of Clerkenwell, exploited commercially by J Lewis Young as an alternative source of power for the Edison wax cylinder phonograph.

The Greenhill Mechanical Phonograph Motor.

THE OPINIONS OF EXPERTS ALL AGREE THAT THIS MOTOR IS PERFECT.

THE GREENHILL MOTOR can be used in any position and at any time.

FOR EXHIBITIONAL PURPOSES it is the only practical method of driving the Phonograph.

FOR BUSINESS PURPOSES it is the solution of the difficulty.

THE GREENHILL MECHANICAL MOTOR will ensure the success of the Phonograph to the user.

SEND FOR PRICE LISTS.

The Greenhill Mechanical Phonograph Motor Co.,
69, FORE STREET, LONDON, E.C.

9 Advertisement for Greenhill's spring motor, 1893

The advent of the graphophone

It was natural that Alexander Graham Bell (1847–1922), the inventor of the telephone, should have been interested in the phonograph, and by 1879 his interest may have been further stimulated by his father-in-law, who, as one of the chief stockholders of the Edison Speaking Phonograph Company, was getting little return on his investment owing to the failure of the imperfect and expensive tinfoil phonograph to retain the interest of the public. His opportunity to take an active part in the development of the instrument came in 1880 when he received from the French Government the Prix Volta that had been established by Napoleon III. In 1879 Bell had set up a laboratory in Washington where he employed Charles Sumner Tainter (1854–1940). They worked there mainly on telephony until Bell's subsidy for this activity came

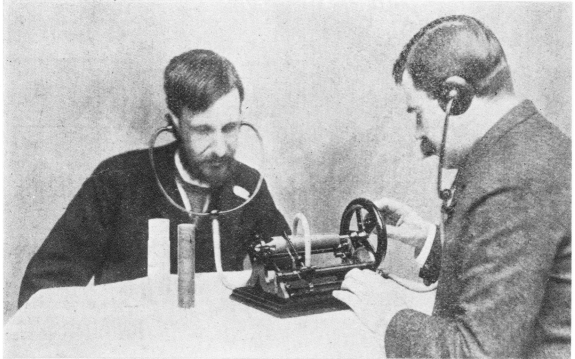

10 C S Tainter listening to the graphophone

11 Bell-Tainter graphophone, 1886

12 Edison perfects the phonograph, 1887–88

incised on the wax-coated surface of a cardboard cylinder. The cylinder did not move linearly as it rotated, but the recorder was moved along it by means of a feed screw. The former improvement was of importance for the future of the talking machine but one wonders why it should have taken four years to complete. The reason was that the Volta associates did not at first confine their investigations entirely to the talking machine, and when they did concentrate on this instrument, after establishing as early as 1881 the feasibility of the wax-incision method by recording on an Edison phonograph whose grooves had been filled with beeswax, they went on to try out almost every type of recorder, recording surface, method of producing relative motion between recorder and surface, and means of reproduction that either occurred to them or could be found in Edison's British Patent 1644 of 1878. For example they tried magnetic recording and also a method in which the sound waves were transmitted through a water jet to the recording diaphragm. They tried both 'hill and dale' recording, in which the vibrations of the recording stylus were perpendicular to the recording surface, and 'lateral cut' in which the vibrations were parallel to the surface. For recording surfaces they tried cylinders, discs and tapes. One method of reproduction

to an end in 1881. The money part of the Prix Volta then enabled him to switch to the development of the talking machine. He now called his research establishment the Volta Laboratory and invited his cousin Chichester Bell (1848–1924) to work there with him.

As regards the talking machine the result of their efforts was revealed in 1885. The principle of their 'graphophone' was substantially the same as that of the phonograph but the sound impressions were

New phonograph

Improved phonograph

Perfected phonograph

that they used was to direct a jet of compressed air at the recorded impressions.

In their work on disc recording Bell and Tainter did not overlook the objection to this method that had occurred both to Cros and Edison, namely that a sound wave of given pitch produces impressions that are more crowded, and therefore more difficult to reproduce, as the stylus approaches the centre of the disc. The solution of this problem requires a mechanism that rotates the disc, not with uniform angular velocity, but in such a way that the reproducing stylus moves relative to the groove surface with constant linear velocity. One of the Bell-Tainter experimental disc mechanisms represents the first of many attempts to solve this problem.

The performance of the Bell-Tainter graphophone was such that it showed distinct promise as a business dictation machine. A tentative approach to officers of the Edison Speaking Phonograph Company with a view to co-operation in its exploitation was understandably rejected. While the Volta Graphophone Company was being organized to hold the relevant patents and the American Graphophone Company to manufacture and distribute the machines, Edison set to work with tremendous energy to improve his invention; the results were, in quick succession, the New Phonograph, the Improved Phonograph and finally the Perfected Phonograph, of which a model suitable for commercial exploitation appeared in June 1888.

The British public had an opportunity of judging the performance of the rival instruments at the British Association meeting in Bath on 6 September 1888, when the phonograph was demonstrated by Edison's agent, Colonel Gouraud, and the graphophone by Henry Edmunds. The essential principles of the two machines were identical; both incised the sound impressions in some form of wax. In the graphophone the wax took the form of a thin layer on a relatively narrow cardboard cylinder, this record

being used once only. In the phonograph the cylinder was wholly of wax and a thick version, not intended for posting, could be used many times over, since the instrument incorporated a shaver to erase a previously recorded impression. Both instruments used separate

13 Graphophone (above) and phonograph (below) as exhibited in England in 1888

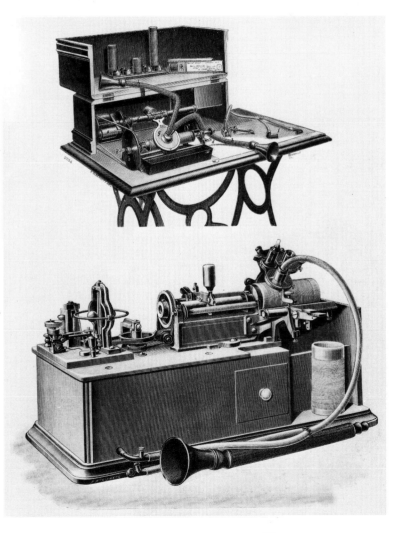

11

recorders and reproducers; in the phonograph the change from one to the other was very conveniently done by rotating through ninety degrees a 'spectacle' device on which they were mounted. Both instruments were intended for use with hearing tubes, though Gouraud was able to use some sort of horn for public demonstrations of the phonograph in small rooms.

As regards the drive the instruments were quite different. The demonstrated model of the graphophone used a treadle mechanism, with an ingenious governor device to keep the speed of rotation reasonably constant. The phonograph used an electric motor. We may now feel inclined to regard this as a point in its favour, but at that time, with the public distribution of electricity in its infancy, the motor had to be driven by a 3-pint bichromate cell with a life of only 15 hours. In spite of the mechanical differences between the two instruments it was the similarity of principle that impressed reporters and the prediction of one of them that lawyers and scientific witnesses would wax fat on this similarity was to be amply fulfilled.

Opinion of the musical possibilities of the two instruments varied widely. One reporter, having sceptically quoted Preece as saying that a Beethoven symphony had been so exquisitely rendered by the machine as to make him shed tears, went on to concede that when it rendered a violin-piano duet he could at least tell when the piano stopped playing. However the American Graphophone Company had been primarily organized by Congress and Supreme Court reporters from Washington to whom the advantages of a dictating machine were obvious, and so it was in this guise that the talking machine made its commercial début.

4
Early exploitation of the talking machine in America

The story of the tortuous manoeuvres that preceded and accompanied the commercial exploitation of the talking machine is too long to be told here and any attempt to abbreviate it is bound to be misleading. It is, however, essential to our purpose to mention that for a time (1888–1894) the phonograph and graphophone interests were harnessed by an arrangement whereby the North American Phonograph Company, organized by the financier J Lippincott, obtained the exclusive agency for the exploitation in the United States of phonographs manufactured by the Edison Phonograph Works, and Lippincott personally gained a similar agency for graphophones manufactured by the American Graphophone Company. He contracted to buy five thousand such instruments a year. Lippincott sub-divided the country into territories and sold to subsidiary companies the exclusive rights to exploit the talking machine within those territories. The instruments were to be hired to customers and not to be sold outright; they were to be maintained by the subsidiary companies and the rental was to be shared between the subsidiaries and the parent.

This enterprise in its original form was a failure. Contributory causes of this failure were initial production difficulties, technical limitations and defects of the instruments, Luddism by stenographers and the prevailing economic depression; the hiring policy has also been blamed, although similar policies were successful before the phonograph venture and have been successful since. But the main reason was that industry was simply not ready for the dictating machine. The telephone, and the typewriter after a slower start, established situations in which a firm that failed to employ them was likely to founder. But for the average firm the use of the dictating machine was at first a luxury, then an alternative to normal stenography and only now is it becoming a necessity.

One thing that became increasingly apparent from 1889 onwards was that if the talking machine was useless in its present form for business it had considerable potentiality for entertainment. An enterprising operator would hire a talking machine and fit it with a device consisting of a U-shaped hollow pipe connected to hearing tubes whereby up to 17 customers could listen to a pre-recorded cylinder. Alternatively the instrument could be made automatic by the addition of a coin-slot mechanism. Suitable records were made either by the operator himself, or by the subsidiary company or by the parent company. Since no reliable means of duplicating records was yet available, it became an arduous matter to meet the demand for pre-recorded cylinders; to produce a batch of 200 records of a march it had to be played 20 times in front of a battery of ten recording horns. It became clear that if the phonograph was to prosper in its new role of public entertainer, the recording process must be centralized, some form of record duplicator must be produced, and the instrument itself must be simplified and cheapened to put it within the reach of the average citizen.

14 An arduous matter But before these new requirements could be met the unnatural alliance of phonograph and graphophone collapsed. The latter instrument had proved to be quite unmarketable. There was never any question of Lippincott being able to fulfil his contract to take five thousand of them a year. Broken in health and bankrupted, he died in 1894. The American Graphophone Company was, however, saved by an alliance with the Columbia Phonograph Company. This, the most successful of the territorial companies, had its origin in an organization which in 1888 had secured the graphophone rights for the District of Columbia, Delaware and Maryland, and which in 1889 was licensed by the North American Phonograph Company to handle the phonograph in the same area. Now

in 1894 the Columbia Phonograph Company (General) was organized to become the distributing agent throughout the world of a projected range of graphophones which were to be improved by the adoption of the most successful features of the phonograph and which would include instruments deliberately designed for home entertainment. Edison, recognizing the inevitability of a similar domestic policy for the phonograph, and suspecting with good cause that his rivals would next attempt to drive him out of business, found himself obliged to enforce the liquidation of the North American Phonograph Company. During the subsequent bankruptcy proceedings he was prevented by law from selling phonographs in the United States (although he could and did continue to export them).

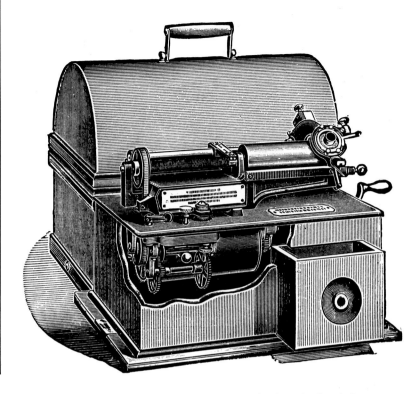

THE BABY GRAND GRAPHOPHONE

Runs with Spring Motor. Weight, 15 lbs. Described in outfit No. 3.

No. 3.

BABY GRAND GRAPHOPHONE.

OUTFIT FOR EXHIBITION OR HOME ENTERTAINMENT.

1 Baby Grand Graphophone; weight, 15 lbs	$75.00
9 records	9.00
3 blanks.............................	.75
3 hearing tubes	3.00
Large horn and stand for concert room	5.50
Canvas case for holding records and tubes........................	6.75
Regular price...................	$100.00

Hence the Columbia Phonograph Company (General) was first in the field in 1894 with a spring driven graphophone suitable for domestic use by those who could afford it. Edison followed as soon as he could; his Spring Motor phonograph was ready in 1896 and it was marketed at $100 by the National Phonograph Company, organized in January of that year.

The Columbia spring motor was not the first to achieve commercial exploitation. A Columbia instrument has been found which has a spring motor by Amet patented in 1892. Two Edison instruments are known, dating from not later than 1894, in which the electric motor has been replaced by an Amet and a Peerless spring motor respectively, both supplied by the Chicago Talking Machine Company. In England the Greenhill motor (see p 8) made a fleeting appearance in 1893 as an alternate source of power for phonographs that were then being supplied (illegally) by a short-lived London distributor. Later in the same year talking dolls appeared in Paris whose vocal mechanism was animated by a spring motor designed by Lioret. (The talking dolls that had been produced between 1887 and 1890 by the Edison Phonograph Toy Manufacturing Company were hand-powered.) The motor that Edison eventually took over for his Spring Motor phonograph had been designed by Capps and marketed by the United States Phonograph Company of Newark.

16 Edison's first Spring Motor phonograph, 1896

left
15 One of the earliest machines marketed with a spring motor, 1895

15

5
Berliner and the gramophone

By 1896, when phonograph and graphophone were poised for an assault on the field of domestic entertainment and on one another, a third competitor had appeared. This was the gramophone, invented by Emile Berliner (1851–1929), who in 1870 emigrated from his native city of Hanover to the United States and, while earning his living in a variety of dead-end jobs, taught himself enough of the subjects of acoustics and electricity to enable him to invent a microphone. This very crude instrument, patented in 1877, was to play an important part in the commercial development of the telephone, but its chief significance to our story lies in the fact that its sale to the Bell Telephone Company and a period of active employment with that company ultimately gave Berliner financial security and the leisure to devote his attention to the problem of the recording and reproduction of sound.

One of Berliner's sources of inspiration was an instrument called the phonautograph, which had been invented in France by Léon Scott de Martinville in 1857 and marketed since 1859 by König, a distinguished acoustician and manufacturer of acoustic instruments. Berliner was familiar with the example of this instrument in the Smithsonian Institution when he lived in Washington; he refers to the 'well-known Phonautograph by Léon Scott'. It consisted of a large horn terminating in a broad membrane, to the centre of which was connected a stylus with the remote end in contact with a sheet of smoke-blackened paper wrapped round the surface of a cylinder having a threaded axle mounted in threaded bearings. When the diaphragm was at rest and the cylinder was rotated

right
17 Emile Berliner

far right
18 Léon Scott's phonautograph, 1857

uniformly the stylus drew a helical white line on the surface of the cylinder. The linkage of stylus and diaphragm was such that when sound waves set the latter in motion the stylus vibrated in a direction parallel to the cylindrical surface and perpendicular to the helix, thus drawing the wave form of the sound. Berliner considered that the uniform resistance of the smoke-blackened surface to the stylus thus moving offered a greater chance of faithful recording than the

17

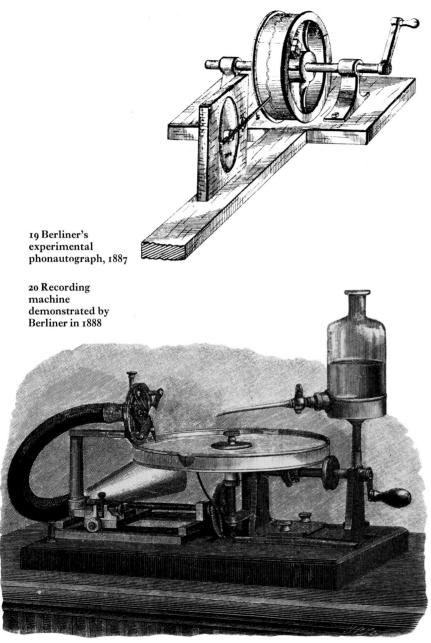

19 Berliner's experimental phonautograph, 1887

20 Recording machine demonstrated by Berliner in 1888

variable resistance offered by a soft surface to a stylus vibrating perpendicularly to the surface. He either wisely ignored or, more probably, had not read the analyses of the performance of this instrument made by academic scientists in Europe, which showed how greatly the wave-form was distorted by resonances of diaphragm and stylus.

Berliner first constructed a very simple form of phonautograph having a narrow drum with no motion of translation as it rotated. He fixed the resulting trace with shellac and was then faced with the problem of converting this into a record suitable for reproduction. Apparently without knowledge of the work of Cros he achieved this by getting a photo-engraver to transform it into an etched groove on a thin metal plate, which he wrapped round the cylinder. The recorder now functioned as reproducer when the stylus was inserted into the groove and the drum was rotated. In further developing this technique Berliner abandoned the cylinder for the disc, to avoid the inconvenience of having first to straighten out the recorded phonautogram for photo-engraving and then to wrap the metal engraving round the cylinder again. In his disc instrument Berliner's recorder traced out a wavy spiral on the under surface of a glass disc which, as it rotated, also moved linearly relative to the fixed stylus. The recording material consisted of a thin layer of lamp-black deposited on a film of linseed oil and it was applied to the lower surface of the disc so that the material removed by recording should drop away from the disc.

Berliner now set out to 'etch the human voice' more directly by eliminating the photographic part of the process. He finally succeeded by a method in which a polished zinc plate was first covered with a solution of beeswax in benzene; evaporation of the benzene left a thin layer of the wax. The recording stylus cut an undulatory spiral into this wax, exposing the metal beneath. Application of a solution of chromic acid etched a corresponding groove in the exposed metal. During the recording process the wax was kept just moistened with alcohol. Berliner found empirically that this prevented dust particles occluded in the wax from adhering, with the swarf, to the stylus. He demonstrated his gramophone before the Franklin Institute at Philadelphia on 16 May 1888 and then began work on the task of evolving some method of reproducing the zinc masters. He interrupted this work in 1889 to visit Germany. In one demonstration, before the Elektrotechnische Verein, the infant gramophone confronted the 'perfected phonograph'. A curious result of this visit to Germany was that the gramophone first became available commercially in the undignified form of a plaything, manufactured by the toy-making firm of Kämmer and Reinhardt of Waltershausen.

It was not until 1893 that the instrument was marketed in the United States. In that year the United States Gramophone Company of Washington began small-scale production, marketing electrically and hand-driven models playing 7″ discs pressed in hard rubber. In 1895 more impetus was achieved by the formation of the Berliner Gramophone Company of Philadelphia to manufacture instruments and 'plates' under licence from the parent company. But it was not until the National Gramophone Company of New York had been organized in 1896 by F Seaman as exclusive sales agency, and the now widely advertised instrument had been provided with a spring motor designed and manufactured by Eldridge R Johnson (1866–1945), that the gramophone became a serious competitor to the phonograph and graphophone. The quality of reproduction was poor and the gramophone made no provision for home recording, but the instrument was relatively cheap, the reproduction was loud (the hearing tubes provided in early models were supplied only to provide 'more natural' reproduction than the horn), and the fact that many plates could

21 Reproducing machine demonstrated by Berliner in 1888

be produced from a single master meant both that they could be sold more cheaply and also that the recording process was less exacting for the performer. Edison remained unimpressed by these advantages but the American Graphophone Company became acutely aware of the threat to its business that they represented.

There followed several years of commercial warfare as complex as it was ruthless, at the end of which the American Graphophone Company, if it had neither destroyed nor enslaved its rival, as at one time seemed possible, had at least gained a foothold in the disc business. We have space to relate only the chief events in this struggle but not to interpret them, which would need a volume. Achievement of the American Graphophone Company's ambition was facilitated by

dissension between the distributing National Gramophone Company (Seaman) and its manufacturers, the Berliner Gramophone Company. The seeds of dissension were sown very early. Seaman was from the start dissatisfied with the financial terms of his contract. The Berliner Gramophone Company, on the other hand, whose contract was with Seaman personally, resented his assignation of his rights to the National Gramophone Company without authority. When negotiations for a European market got under way Seaman suspected, probably correctly, that he would be squeezed out of them.

The progress of the dissension was marked by the appearance of the word Zon-o-phone and its changing significance. Originally (early 1898) it was a name under which Seaman, in defiance of one of the terms

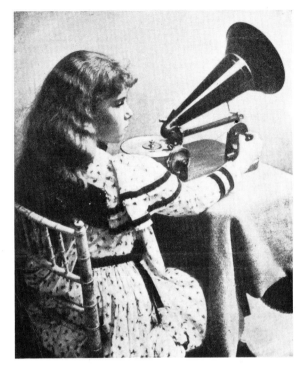

24 A child could use it

25 Eldridge
R Johnson, founder
of the Victor Talking
Machine Company

in his contract, advertised Berliner gramophones until forbidden to do so. Some months later it re-emerged as the name of a coin-slot version of the Berliner gramophone, manufactured by a Seaman creature called the Universal Talking Machine Company. Finally (mid 1899) it appeared as the name of a domestic instrument, with records, in full scale production at the New York factory of this same company. Soon afterwards Seaman's orders for Berliner gramophones, now manufactured completely by Johnson, dried up. A Seaman advertisement of November 1900 refers to the 'Zon-o-phone (substituted for our Gram-o-phone which is abandoned)'.

Meanwhile Seaman's National Gramophone Company (later Corporation) had been under legal attack since late 1898 by the American Graphophone Company for alleged infringement of the Bell-Tainter patents. In early 1900 they suddenly settled for an injunction by consent, ie they admitted that the Berliner gramophone was an infringement. Dealing in the gramophone by the Berliner Gramophone Company was brought to a halt while that in the Zonophone continued under license. Johnson, however, formed his own company (called initially the Consolidated Talking Machine Company) so as to continue in business, which by now included a substantial commitment to the European market. Surviving an attempt by the American Graphophone Company to put a stop to this, but forbidden to use the name gramophone, he called his instrument the Victor Talking Machine. Eventually, in October 1901, the Berliner and Johnson interests were united under

21

the management of Johnson as the Victor Talking Machine Company.

But Johnson was by now using a process in which the recording was carried out, not by the etched plate method, but by incising a groove of constant depth in the surface of a thick wax blank. The recorded surface was then rendered electrically conducting and a metallic negative was deposited on it by electrolysis. This negative was then used for stamping the records, using now the shellac-based material that had been introduced in 1897. Johnson had not patented the original recording process, but an application for such a patent had been made in 1897 by J Jones, who had worked for a time in Berliner's laboratory, keeping his eyes wide open. Four years later the patent was granted: it was immediately bought by the American Graphophone Company and by late 1901 the company was manufacturing the 'Disc Graphophone'.

Eventually it became clear that with Victor allegedly infringing the Jones patent and the American Graphophone Company the Berliner patents, a state of deadlock had been reached for which the only solution was an agreement to pool patents. Thus by 1902 there was established in the United States a situation in which the exploitation of the talking machine was in the hands of three companies, with Edison's National Phonograph Company supplying only cylinder instruments, the Victor Talking Machine Company supplying only disc instruments and the Columbia Phonograph Company supplying both kinds, which were manufactured by the American Graphophone Company.

The fact that Columbia's first discs had been manufactured under the name Climax by the Globe Record Company, which had been bought and then made over to Columbia by Johnson of all people, is but one example of the complexities concealed by the simplified story given in this chapter. Another twist in the story that has not been followed here concerns the brief appearance in 1899/1900 of the Vitaphone (with its red discs) whose manufacture by the American Talking Machine Company was instigated by the American Graphophone Company as an element of its campaign against Berliner.

6
The talking machine industry in Great Britain

The right to exploit the improved phonograph in Europe was originally assigned by Edison to Colonel Gouraud (?1842–1912), an American Civil War veteran with a flair for publicity, who had been previously active in the promotion of Edison's telephone and electric light interests. Gouraud used his social connections to arrange demonstrations at which persons prominent in church, state and the arts were persuaded to record their voices for posterity, and he sent out representatives to give lectures in the

26 Colonel Gouraud listens to a message recorded by Edison, 1888

provinces. To the London demonstrations we owe the cylinders on which have survived the recorded voices of Gladstone, Browning and others.

As regards the peripatetic lecturers, J L Young, manager and shareholder of the Edison Phonograph Company, reminiscing in 1913, asserted that their

27 Programme of a phonograph entertainment at Bradford, 1889

prime function was to subsidize with their takings the payment of the costly fees for taking out Edison's 'multiplicity of imbecile patents' in Europe. These lecturers could hardly have been salesmen since Young, writing in June 1890, found himself obliged to pose and answer the question 'why had it (the phonograph) not been put on the market in this country ?'. In the same year the phonograph was described, in the *Illustrated London News*, as an instrument 'much more often talked about than into'.

By this time, as a corollary of events in the USA already described, the promoting company had become the London branch of the Edison United Phonograph Company, which had been established in 1890 in the USA to control the patents of both phonograph and graphophone outside North America. In 1892 the Edison Bell Phonograph Corporation Ltd was set up to acquire the British patents. The policy adopted by this corporation was to hire phonographs at a rental of £10 per annum for use as office dictation machines; a few instruments called Drawing Room Phonographs were also hired for the same fee, but they were supplied without the recording device. At first this policy met with some success and about 700 machines were hired, but after a few years the rate at which they were returned began to exceed the rate of new hirings.

Before the establishment of this corporation a few talking machines had entered this country to be sold outright to showmen. The new licensing arrangements failed to check this practice, and among those who engaged in it was J E Hough (1848–1925) who set up the London Phonograph Company and started to make records. He was, with others including J L Young, duly sued by Edison-Bell. The proceedings dragged on for months, but the supply of phonographs to Hough continued unchecked. In an entertaining speech made at a celebration of his 70th birthday (1918) Hough referred with relish to this period of his rumbustious career. He mentioned phonographs that were sold 'on the quay' and some that, with their reproducers separately packed and despatched, entered this country as 'planing machines'. He did not mention the origin of his phonographs but it seems likely that they came from local subsidiaries of the North American Phonograph Company.

Eventually an agreement was reached whereby Hough obtained the right to sell phonographs for domestic entertainment and for public performances while Edison Bell retained control of the instrument as an office dictation machine. Hough now (1897) established the firm of Edisonia Limited and, having acquired some record duplicators from America, enjoyed a brief independent existence as a legitimate supplier of phonographs and records. In 1898, however, the Edison Bell concern was reorganized as the Edison Bell Consolidated Phonograph Company; Edisonia's license was given up to this firm for a consideration and Edisonia became its manufactory and a sales outlet. The cylinders first produced were called London Records; later came names such as Standard, Popular, Grand Concert, Indestructible and Indestructible Ebony. After a moulding process had been devised a factory was acquired in Peckham in 1903 for the manufacture of 'gold moulded' records and of phonographs.

The first major challenge to the Edison Bell monopoly came from the gramophone. In mid-1897 W B Owen, who had been a director of the National Gramophone Company (Seaman) when it was formed, came to England with the primary object of negotiating the sale or lease of the Berliner patents in Europe and the secondary one of testing the British market for Seaman by himself trading in instruments and records shipped from America. Berliner himself visited Germany to investigate possibilities there. Negotiations were complicated by the dissension that was going on in America (p 20) but the ultimate

CAUTION.

We deem it to be our duty to respectfully warn the public against purchasing or using any Phonograph or Graphophone which has not attached to it a license plate issued by us and bearing our name, "EDISONIA Limited," as well as the registered number of the machine prominently embossed upon it.

There have been serious legal actions as referred to on the first page, which have fully established the patent rights of the Edison Bell Phonograph Corporation Ltd., of whom we are the Sole Licensees, and Authorised Vendors. Any machine sold or purchased from any other source, renders its purchaser as well as the seller, liable to legal procedure.

result was the establishment in April 1898 of the Gramophone Company by Owen and a group headed by Trevor Williams. The Company acquired an exclusive license to manufacture and sell records and instruments in the UK and to sell in the rest of the world excluding North America. The original headquarters of the company was a modest establishment in Maiden Lane, Strand, London, where a recording studio was set up and instruments supplied by Eldridge Johnson (not through Seaman) were assembled. Negotiations for a pressing plant in England failed; eventually this was set up in Hanover by the Deutsche Grammophon Gesellschaft, a company which was capitalized by three Berliner brothers, Emile, Jacob and Joseph, directed by Joseph, and originally operated in a corner of Joseph's telephone factory. The story of the rise of the Gramophone Company to a position of pre-eminence in the talking machine industry is resumed in a later chapter. It is sufficient to mention that the inevitable legal attack by Edison Bell, preceded by threatening letters to dealers who sold gramophones, was settled out of court for quite a modest sum.

28 Edison Bell protects its monopoly

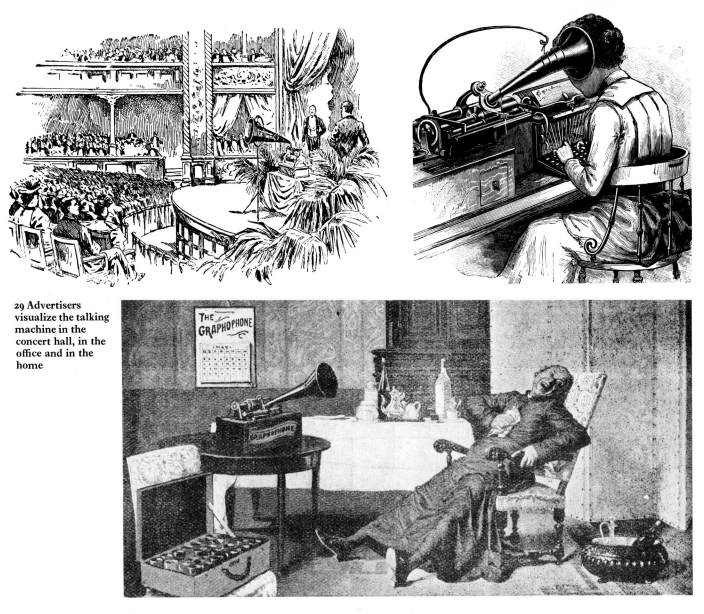

29 Advertisers visualize the talking machine in the concert hall, in the office and in the home

26

The basic patents acquired by Edison Bell expired between 1900 and 1903. The Columbia Phonograph Company, which set up its European headquarters in Paris in 1897, established a sales office in London in 1899, and shifted its headquarters to London in 1900. Edison's National Phonograph Company set up its European headquarters in Antwerp in 1897; recording started in London in 1902 and the European headquarters was established there in 1904. The French firm that almost monopolized the talking machine industry in France appeared in London in 1902 as Pathé Frères (London) Ltd. Zonophones, exported from America, appeared in England in 1899, to the indignation of the Gramophone Company which threatened to confiscate them. Eventually the International Zonophone Company was established in Berlin (1901) to control the sales of Zonophones in Europe, with a subsidiary, the British Zonophone Company, in London. These companies had a very brief independent life, however, for they were bought by the Gramophone and Typewriter Ltd in 1903. The name survived, however, on Zonophone instruments and discs at 'popular' prices that enabled G & T to gain a share of the mass market without sacrificing its reputation for quality.

The talking machine industry was closely concentrated in the City Road area of London. Instruments and records were distributed to dealers either directly or through factors such as Barnett Samuel and Sons Ltd, an old-established musical instrument firm which entered the phonograph field in 1901 and ultimately manufactured instruments under the name Decca. Although the industry was an expanding one the dealer did not automatically prosper. Being engaged in a luxury trade he was among the first to suffer during a year of business depression such as 1909. He had to accept the fact that the business was highly seasonal; sales of instruments rose from September to December then dropped almost to zero.

Sales of records continued after Christmas but fell away during the summer. To contend with this the dealer often sold bicycles as well, an arrangement which was commercially sound, but was not approved by critics who considered that a cycle engineer might lack the musical sensitivity required of a talking machine dealer. The dealer also had to contend with price cutting. The major companies established resale price maintenance and enforced it as well as they could, but this rebounded on any dealer who overstocked records and was not allowed to dispose of them at cut prices. Dealers also suffered from the

30 W B Owen, who introduced the gramophone into England

27

31 The gramophone
dealer often sold
bicycles as well

price war between the record manufacturers as a
result of which the retail price of the popular cylinder
dropped from 1s6d to 9d in the period under dis-
cussion and that of the popular 10″ disc from 4s0d
(single-sided) to 1s0d (double-sided). Finally a sucess-
ful dealer had to show a nice judgement in his choice
of instruments. Gramophones could be sold successfully in a prosperous residential area; only cheap
German instruments could be sold in a working-class
area, but in intermediate situations the choice of wares
required considerable acumen.

A bewildering variety of imports from Germany
entered this country between 1900 and 1914. In some
cases the German firm sold instruments directly to
dealers through an agency in this country. Thus Fritz
Puppel sold a range of cheap cylinder and disc instruments through the agent M and A Wolff. It was
usually considered desirable to give such instruments
reassuringly patriotic names; thus a group of instruments exported in 1907 by a Leipzig firm through the
New Polyphon Supply Company were called Monarch,
Baron, Marquis, Regina etc. In other cases instruments wholly made in Germany were marketed by a
British factor, who did not necessarily indicate the
origin of his wares. Thus the factor Murdoch sold
instruments supplied by the German firm of Excelsior.
Again a British firm might import all components from
abroad (except some that were patented locally) and
supply its own cabinets. Finally a British firm that
proudly proclaimed that all its instruments were
British-made might import motors from Germany or
Switzerland and justify its claim by identifying the
terms 'make' and 'assemble'. Hence in addition to
the families of instruments supplied by the Gramophone Company (including Zonophones), Edison,
Edison Bell, Columbia and Pathé, other families were
established such as Barnett Samuel's Dulcephones,
Murdoch's Tournaphones, Craies and Stavridi's
Apollos, and Lockwood's Perophones, whose con-

tinental affinity could be suspected even if it was not explicitly stated.

During the period 1900–1914 approximately 60 different types of needle-cut discs, 10 phono-cut discs and 30 cylinders were marketed in Great Britain. The cylinder trade was at first dominated by Edison, Edison Bell, Columbia and Pathé, but a crisis in the industry occurred between 1905 and 1907 when the introduction of five new types (Rex, Sterling, White, London Popular, Clarion) swamped a market that had already begun to dwindle. Of these Sterling at 1s0d achieved some considerable initial success in 1906, aided by an advertising campaign that included a balloon flight over London, but it was defeated by the reduction in price of Edison cylinders from 1s6d to 1s0d and the introduction of the Clarion cylinder at 9d in autumn 1907. The unpretentious Clarion, together with Edison's Blue Amberol and the cylinders issued by the Indestructible Record Company of Albany, shared the distinction of being the only cylinders that survived into the Great War period, since Pathé abandoned the cylinder trade in 1906, Columbia did so in 1910 and Edison Bell in 1913.

The disc market was ultimately to be dominated by the black, shellac-based needle-cut disc 10″ or 12″ in diameter, recorded on both sides. The Gramophone and Typewriter Ltd introduced a 10″ disc in 1901 and a 12″ disc in 1903, and European record buyers first became aware of discs recorded on both sides in 1904 when they were issued under the Odeon label by the International Talking Machine Company of Berlin. (These were not, however, the first discs to be so pressed; a few discs of the Berliner type had been experimentally recorded on both sides in 1900 by Johnson in America and towards the end of its brief independent life the International Zonophone Company had issued a few such discs for one of its agencies.)

But there was to be much experiment in colour,

32 A dealer laments
the price war, 1907

The MAGNET.

The EXCELSIOR.

The ANGELICA.

LA FAVORITA.

The ANGELUS.

TOURNAPHONE
MODEL
A.

The SYLVIA C.

The PANDORA.

L' ENCHANTRESSE.

The BABY
TOURNAPHONE.

33 German
instruments
marketed in
England, 1906

TOURNAPHONE
MODEL
H.

TOURNAPHONE
MODEL
K.

materials, type of cut and size before standardization was affected. Thus the 'unbreakable' brown Nicole disc, introduced in 1903, was ultimately a commercial failure, as was also the white Neophone phono-cut disc having an enamel surface on a backing of compressed paper, which survived, with periodic reorganization of the manufacturing company, from 1904 to 1908. The Pathé firm, when it abandoned the cylinder for the disc in 1906, also used the phono-cut; the recording started at the middle rather than at the outside of the disc, and was played with a sapphire stylus instead of a steel needle. In the hands of Pathé the phono-cut was technically successful and the firm's needle-cut disc (the Actuelle) did not appear in England until 1921.

The first imported German disc, the Odeon, was followed by the Beka, Favorite, Homophon, Jumbo and others. Competition forced the price down; for a double-sided needle-cut 10″ disc it was 5s0d in 1904 and 2s6d in 1909, at which figure it stabilized for a period. Rena records at this price were then being pressed for the Rena Manufacturing Company from Columbia masters on Columbia presses but in late 1909 it was announced that Columbia had taken over the record business of this company and would from then on issue its double-sided discs on the Rena label at the Rena price. The Gramophone Company appeared to stand aside from this competition. Its prices remained high and it did not issue double-sided discs under its own name in England until 1912 but in fact it made its contribution to cheapening the disc by establishing in 1908 the Twin Record Company to manufacture the 'half crown disc'.

The next overt event in the price war occurred early in 1912 when J E Hough Ltd (formerly Edison Bell) introduced the Winner record at 1s6d. Hough later asserted that this was done in order to cope with the plethora of cheap German discs that had entered the market. Judging only by list prices these German discs were no cheaper than their British competitors but it appears that there was little relationship between the list price and the price at which the disc was actually sold. Some German manufacturers reacted to the Winner by dropping their list prices to 1s 6d but consternation was reported from Germany when in 1913 the Gramophone Company introduced its (Zonophone) Cinch at 1s 1d and Columbia its Phoenix, also at 1s 1d. The last word before the guns began to fire was said by the German firm whose discs could be bought at 10½d.

The talking machine industry was well served then, as is its counterpart today, by its specialized press. The *Talking Machine News* (established 1903) *Phonotrader and Recorder* (1904) and *Sound Wave*

(1907) formed valuable links between manufacturers, dealers and the public; in them editorial integrity was stubbornly maintained sometimes against strong pressure by aggrieved advertisers. Serious musical criticism centred on gramophone records first appeared regularly from 1906 in the German *Phonographische Zeitschrift*; in England it did not achieve the high standard of scholarship and style that we now take for granted in serious gramophone journals until the establishment of the *Gramophone* in 1923. Technical criticism, nowadays exercised by skilled engineers with a gift for popularization, then appeared largely in the correspondence columns and the only qualification needed for indulging in it seems to have been enthusiasm.

Colonel Gouraud's counterpart in Germany and Austria as publicist for Edison's phonograph was Dr Theodor Wangemann. The highlights of his tour were demonstrations given to Bismarck and to the young Kaiser Wilhelm II in 1889. A phonograph was delivered to the Imperial Court via Werner Siemens in 1890 and another recipient of Edison's largesse was Friedrich Krupp, who was given a model powered by a water motor. An English dealer, Mr John Nottingham, reminiscing in 1906, said that he was running a successful phonograph business in Berlin in 1894 but he eventually had to return to England when the patent rights were allotted to Gebrüder Stollwerck. Stollwerck made little use of these rights, finding them less valuable than was expected and by 1900, when the patents were about to expire, they were in the hands of the Deutsche Edison Gesellschaft who were later asserted to have produced copies of Edison phonographs that were too few and too unreliable to create a market.

A local industry was initiated, however, by A Költzow, who claimed to have been making phonographs in 1890, and by W Bahre, who started in 1892. When publicly demonstrating a phonograph of his own design in 1894 Költzow was emphatic in asserting that its primary purpose was to replace the stenographer but in the following year he and Bahre designed an instrument especially for the travelling showman. Importation of the cheaper Columbia domestic graphophones in 1898 was followed by the appearance of some locally manufactured imitations. The Excelsior firm, founded in 1899, produced a

series of instruments with this Columbia affinity which were imported into England and were still being sold by the factor Murdoch as late as 1911 when all other cylinder instruments, apart from Edison's, had vanished from the market.

In Germany as in England the errant Zonophone (p 21) enjoyed but a brief independent existence. Originally (1899) F M Prescott, export agent for the National Gramophone Company, distributed Zonophones in Germany through the firm of Bumb und König (who later manufactured Beka records). Subsequently (1901) Prescott organized the International Zonophone Company of Berlin to conduct the European business. The inevitable legal conflict was duly initiated by the Deutsche Grammophon Aktiengesellschaft but eventually (1903) the English parent company extinguished this competition by buying the Zonophone business. They bought it without Prescott, however, and he immediately (1903) went on to establish the International Talking Machine Company to manufacture instruments and discs under the name Odeon.

The most remarkable contribution of the Germans to the infant phonograph industry was the celebrated Puck instrument. Built on a cast-iron lyre-shaped base, it had an exposed single-spring motor with a governor and a partially balanced horn connected at the throat to a reproducer which moved across the cylinder as the latter rotated. The starting lever and speed control were combined so that the owner had to start the instrument and use the first few bars of the music to adjust the speed to a reasonable value;

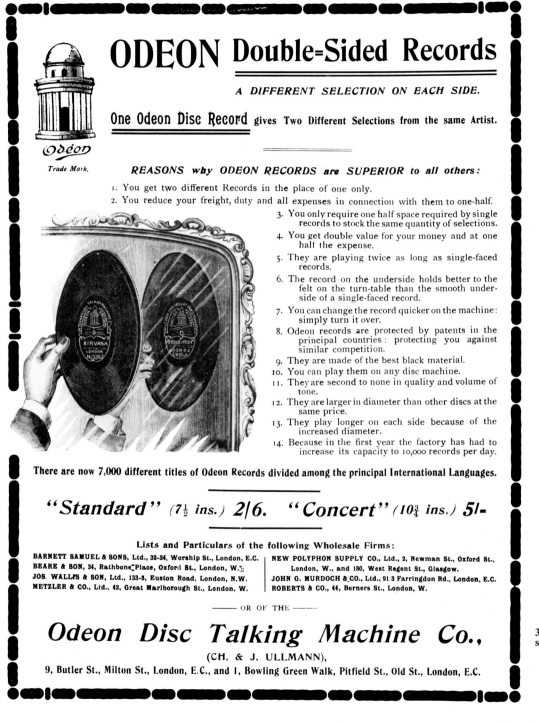

ODEON Double=Sided Records

A DIFFERENT SELECTION ON EACH SIDE.

One Odeon Disc Record gives Two Different Selections from the same Artist.

Odeon
Trade Mark.

REASONS why ODEON RECORDS are SUPERIOR to all others:

1. You get two different Records in the place of one only.
2. You reduce your freight, duty and all expenses in connection with them to one-half.
3. You only require one half space required by single records to stock the same quantity of selections.
4. You get double value for your money and at one half the expense.
5. They are playing twice as long as single-faced records.
6. The record on the underside holds better to the felt on the turn-table than the smooth underside of a single-faced record.
7. You can change the record quicker on the machine: simply turn it over.
8. Odeon records are protected by patents in the principal countries : protecting you against similar competition.
9. They are made of the best black material.
10. You can play them on any disc machine.
11. They are second to none in quality and volume of tone.
12. They are larger in diameter than other discs at the same price.
13. They play longer on each side because of the increased diameter.
14. Because in the first year the factory has had to increase its capacity to 10,000 records per day.

There are now 7,000 different titles of Odeon Records divided among the principal International Languages.

"Standard" (7½ ins.) 2/6. "Concert" (10¾ ins.) 5/-

Lists and Particulars of the following Wholesale Firms:

BARNETT SAMUEL & SONS, Ltd., 32-34, Worship St., London, E.C.
BEARE & SON, 34, Rathbone Place, Oxford St., London, W.
JOS. WALLIS & SON, Ltd., 133-5, Euston Road, London, N.W.
METZLER & CO., Ltd., 42, Great Marlborough St., London, W.

NEW POLYPHON SUPPLY CO., Ltd., 2, Newman St., Oxford St., London, W., and 180, West Regent St., Glasgow.
JOHN G. MURDOCH & CO., Ltd., 91/3 Farringdon Rd., London, E.C.
ROBERTS & CO., 44, Berners St., London, W.

—— OR OF THE ——

Odeon Disc Talking Machine Co.,

(CH. & J. ULLMANN),

9, Butler St., Milton St., London, E.C., and 1, Bowling Green Walk, Pitfield St., Old St., London, E.C.

34 Odeon uses both sides of the disc, 1904

35 Puck instruments
a) Early model
b) Lyra model with
flower horn, 1905
c) Lohengrin model
(Kastenpuck), 1905
d) Lorelei model,
1906
e) model for both
cylinders and discs,
1905

34

the performance usually ended with the horn falling off the end of the cylinder. No feed-screw was necessary since the instrument was not intended for recording. It appears to have been invented by W Bahre, who may have been inspired by cylinder instruments without feed-screws designed by Lioret in France (1896) and by Bettini in America (1897). Hundreds of thousands of these simple instruments were manufactured by firms such as Carl Lindström (founded 1896) and sold locally and in England at prices (eg 3s 6d in England) which must have given manufacturer and retailer little or no profit. Their sale continued because it stimulated the sale of cylinders and because it was hoped that their purchasers would ultimately aspire to higher things. Sometimes the Puck was subjected to the indignity of being given away free to a purchaser of a number of cylinders. It could not at first be sold in America because American courts were likely to look more severely on its possession of a tapered mandrel – an Edison patent – than had the German courts, but it was at one time employed by Columbia to boost its declining cylinder trade.

Inspired by a love-hate relationship towards this exasperating instrument the German manufacturers continued to develop it. The brake and speed adjustment were separated; it was provided with levelling screws and spirit levels; it was modified so as to play Grand size cylinders; it acquired a flower horn. Mounted on a wooden box it became a Kastenpuck. An instrument capable of playing both cylinders and discs made a fleeting appearance. On one model (Syrena) a seductive syren modified the severity of the cast-iron base; on another (Lorelei) there was a figure representing the Lorelei legend. Some models were provided with feed-screw mechanisms and so could be used for recording. Whatever the refinements the Puck remained cheap, and although this term is often used pejoratively in accounts of early German

contributions to the development of the talking machine it cannot be denied that the Puck gave pleasure to millions who could not otherwise have profited by Edison's invention.

The cylinder instrument was, however, shortlived in Germany as elsewhere. An attempt by the Edison Company to enforce its moulding patents, just when the disc instrument was gaining in popularity, was legitimate and initially successful, but it accelerated the decline of the cylinder by encouraging German manufacturers to concentrate on cheapening the disc to regain their lost mass market.

The Deutsche Grammophon Aktiengesellschaft (DGA), came to occupy in Germany much the same position as its British parent, the Gramophone Company. It dominated the quality market with products under its own name while using the Zonophone label to compete for the mass market with sufficient success to be accused of aiming at a monopoly by ruining its competitors when, in 1913, it dropped the price of a double-sided 10″ disc to the equivalent of 1s 3d. Its arch enemy in the market place and in the courts was the firm of Carl Lindström, which, by a series of amalgamations, built up an enormous local and foreign trade in instruments and motors and, by 1913, controlled the sale of Beka, Dacapo, Favorite, Fonotipia, Lyrophon, Jumbo and Odeon records as well as its own Parlophons. The major technical developments in the disc machine during this period were the introduction of the tapered tone arm with a rotatable soundbox, and of the 'hornless' instrument. The latter was a German innovation, but the English-owned DGA gained control of the relevant patent; hence, in the period 1903–1914, German ingenuity was concentrated aggressively on the techniques of mass production for cheapness and defensively on attempts to circumvent the restrictive patents. In 1912, after years of litigation, Lindström agreed to pay a licence fee for their use, but this was

**36 Puck entertains
the family**

not to be the end of the matter, since at the Leipzig spring fair, in the following year, DGA created a sensation by confiscating the hornless machines exhibited by the Anker, Kalliope, Excelsior, Allegro, Polyphon, Favorite and Prettner firms.

The German talking machine industry was concentrated at Berlin and at Leipzig and its products were demonstrated to the world at the Leipzig spring and autumn fairs, of which the former was the more important since it was attended by foreign merchants who came to buy for the following Christmas season and to encourage the continual fall of prices by playing off one manufacturer against the other. One characteristic German product which failed to impress the English buyer was the automat. Before the advent of the domestic talking machine there had grown up in Leipzig a mechanical music industry, supplying musical boxes of all kinds, mechanical pianos and orchestrions, many of them actuated by coinslot mechanisms. Faced with competition from the talking machine, some of the firms affected replied by taking up the manufacture of the latter. With examples from Edison, Columbia and DGA before them they had little difficulty in making them suitable for coinslot operation to play a single record, but by the time they had solved the technical problems of record selection and change of needle their market was crippled by a tax on automatic music. For a time, however, the automats flourished and they received a new impetus through the advent of the loudspeaking talking machines to which we shall refer later. Few of these instruments reached England, however, possibly owing to different social habits in the two countries.

Another aspect of the German talking machine industry which was looked upon without favour by English buyers was a vein of lyricism which expressed itself in the styling of the instrument. The horn flowered modestly in England; in Germany it did so with tropical abandon. Although Holzweissig's

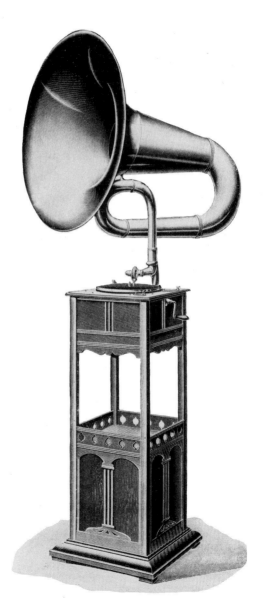

37 **Exalting the horn; Olymp 21, a typical German automat, 1910**

37

38 Concealing the horn; the Hymnophon (1909 model of the instrument introduced in 1904)

right
39 Disguising the horn, 1906

Hymnophon of 1904 indicated the right way to conceal the horn, later manufacturers merely disguised it. The instrument went into a box and the horn masqueraded above it as a majolica group, a lighthouse or a windmill. One complete instrument took the form of a potted plant, and another that of a Greek temple. Holzweissig produced a hornless instrument in the shape of an upright beer barrel and another model appeared as a flowered grotto with coloured lights and a fountain which played when the record was started. These extravagances were, of course, exceptional, but we have already seen the same tendency at work on mass-produced instruments such as the Lorelei Puck and it appears also in the elaborately detailed metallic plates which were fixed, first to the more expensive disc instruments and then to the cheaper ones.

left
40 Debasing the horn; Hymnophon Fass-Automat, 1909

below
41 Embellishing the horn; Parlophon Automat Junior, 1912

Edison phonographs in Great Britain

By the time the European headquarters of the National Phonograph Company moved to London in 1904 it was distributing both cylinders made in America and also those recorded in London and moulded in the Antwerp factory. Both National and Columbia had multiplied productivity of cylinders in 1902 by substituting a moulding process for that of mechanical duplication. Edison at first used a sputtered film of gold to prepare the master cylinder for the receipt of an electrolytic deposit, and he described the resultant cylinders as 'gold moulded'. Edison's competitors adopted the same sales-stimulating term, but in some cases it is doubtful whether the masters ever encountered an atom of gold since the humbler element carbon, in the form of powdered graphite, was found to be equally effective.

The instruments to play these records, no longer distributed exclusively by Edison Bell, included the Triumph (introduced as the Spring Motor in 1896), the Home (1896) the Standard (1898) and the Gem (1899). They are here listed in descending order of price and performance; the Triumph had a triple spring and played 14 cylinders at one winding while the Gem had a single spring playing only two cylinders. The Concert phonograph, which played wax records of 5″ diameter, and which Edison had reluctantly introduced in 1899 to meet the challenge of the similar Graphophone Grand, was by now obsolescent. In addition there came a trickle of other instruments including electrically driven models for either battery or mains drive (eg the Victor or the Conqueror) and coin-operated models (eg Ajax and

Bijou). Models with AC mains motors (eg Alva) did not appear until 1907.

The instruments of the Triumph-Gem family were well designed, well constructed and, with the exception of the comparatively fragile reproducer, robust. Many have survived until today, in perfect working order. In 1907 another instrument was added to the range, called at first the Ideal and then the Idelia; with oxidized bronze metal fittings it was the most expensive of the group, designed 'to fulfil the requirements of every home, no matter how handsomely furnished'. Minor changes were made in these instruments almost every year, so that it is easy to date a particular model, but the major changes in the distant external appearance of the models arose from the substitution, in 1908, for the straight trumpet hitherto supplied, of a segmented horn supported by a crane, and, in 1910, of an upright 'Cygnet' horn.

A much more important but less conspicuous change occurred in late 1908, when Edison introduced a cylinder called the Amberol, having 200 grooves to the inch and playing for four minutes, to supplement the standard cylinder with 100 grooves to the inch and playing for two minutes. To play the new record 'combination' instruments were marketed, having a gear-change lever whereby the speed of traverse of the reproducer across the cylinder could be halved, and provided with two reproducers, one for each type of cylinder. These new instruments lacked the end-gate which was opened to put the cylinder on the mandrel – a conspicuous feature of earlier models. Attachments were also sold whereby owners of

opposite
42 Some Edison cylinder phonographs of the period 1896–1912

TRIUMPH
Model A

TRIUMPH
Model B

TRIUMPH
Model C and D

TRIUMPH
Model E, F and G

OPERA

STANDARD
Model A

STANDARD
Model B

STANDARD
Model C and D

STANDARD
Model E, F and G

BALMORAL
Model M and E

HOME
Model A and B

HOME
Model C and D

IDELIA
Model D1

IDELIA
Model D2

GEM
Model A

GEM
Model B and C

GEM
Model D and E

HOME
Model E, F and G

FIRESIDE
Model A

FIRESIDE
Model B

43 Edison Concert phonograph; 1902 version of model introduced in 1899

existing instruments could convert them to play the new cylinders. A new instrument, called the Fireside phonograph, was added to the range in 1909, intermediate in price between Gem and Standard. This instrument was equipped with a single reproducer having a double stylus and a swivel device to engage the one appropriate to the type of cylinder in use. The last of the exposed horn phonographs, called at first the Opera and later the Concert, was introduced in England in 1912; it was for four-minute cylinders only and in it the reproducer remained stationary while the rotating cylinder moved linearly past it. The sound emerged from an elegant, self-supported wooden horn. All exposed-horn models sold after October 1912 played only four-minute cylinders and in autumn 1913 the manufacture of such models ceased.

Meanwhile the National Phonograph Company had met the demand for an enclosed horn phonograph with an instrument called the Amberola, introduced in 1909. By 1913 seven models were available, Nos I, III, IV being of the cabinet type and Nos V, VI, VIII, X being table models. By 1915 the range had been reduced to three, called the 30, 50 and 75 in accordance with their price in dollars in the USA, together with the older model V. In 1912 a new type of cylinder called the Blue Amberol, was introduced. It had a plastic surface on a plaster of Paris backing, and was played with a reproducer having a diamond stylus instead of the sapphire type hitherto used. But by this time the cylinder had long ceased to be a serious competitor to the disc, as Edison reluctantly recognized when he introduced his disc phonograph.

Edison's dealers as well as his competitors sometimes complained vociferously about his business methods, but there is every reason to believe that his customers were satisfied. They paid moderate prices for excellent instruments, and there was no question of built-in obsolescence, since whenever an improvement was introduced, provision was made to incor-

44 a) Edison Opera (later Concert) phonograph, 1912

44 b) Edison advertises the Concert phonograph

EDISON CONCERT PHONOGRAPH

MAHOGANY

Price, £18-18-0

Cabinet, Mahogany, piano finish, with cover. Diamond Point Reproducer Model A. Self-supported mahogany wood cygnet horn. Noiseless automatic stop. Double spring, direct drive motor; can be wound while playing.

Plays Blue Amberol Records only, but will play any four-minute record when equipped with a Sapphire Point Reproducer.

Size (without horn), 14¾ inches high; 18 inches wide; 12¾ inches deep.

Same instrument with oak cabinet (without handles) and oak horn, £17-17-0

porate it into older instruments. They had to be content with a somewhat humble level of entertainment, consisting of military band selections, xylophone and cornet solos, ballads, coon songs, comic recitations etc, for Edison's grand opera records of 1906 could not satisfy a serious musician, since they were of only two minutes duration, and his grand opera Amberols of 1910 and the concert cylinders of 1912, designed, like the discs, 'to appeal to the head rather than to the heart and the heels' failed to regain an audience which had already deserted the cylinder for the disc. But there still remained a band of devoted and enthusiastic cylinder lovers, equipped with instruments which, when carefully maintained, seemed immortal, and Edison continued to supply them with cylinders until 1929.

In the early days of competition between cylinder and disc instruments one of the chief selling points of the former had been the fact that they made provision for home recording. The Standard, Home and Triumph models were sold with recorders and included a device whereby the surface of the wax blank supplied for home recording could be shaved. This was successful only in the hands of a skilled and patient user and failed to work at all on the gateless models of 1909, from which it was therefore omitted. When an attempt was made in 1912 to revive the art of home recording a separate shaving machine was supplied. An office dictation machine called the Business Phonograph was introduced in 1906. In 1929, when Edison left the entertainment field, the manufacture of 'Ediphones' continued and the cylinder phonograph finished its career, as it had begun it, in the form of a dictation machine, still competing as vigorously as ever with the sole surviving descendant of the cylinder graphophone, known as the Dictaphone.

The Gramophone Company, which had been established in London in 1898, marketed a 7″ disc which was recorded on one side only and bore as a trade mark the figure of a recording angel. The famous 'dog and trumpet' trade mark was acquired in 1899, when the artist Francis Barraud called at the Maiden Lane office to borrow a brass horn so that he might revise a picture of a fox terrier listening to an Edison Bell Commercial phonograph which he had painted some years before. W B Owen, the managing director of the Gramophone Company, offered to buy the picture, provided that the phonograph was painted out and a gramophone was substituted. The new trade mark was at first used more vigorously by Eldridge Johnson in America than it was in England where it first appeared on records in 1909; it was not until 1910, after the Gramophone Company had failed to establish in the courts its exclusive right to the use of the word 'gramophone', that it was decided to exploit the trade mark as fully as possible. The gramophone met with public favour from the start; nevertheless W B Owen thought it wise to diversify the activities of the company and in 1900 it was reorganized as the Gramophone and Typewriter Ltd to sell the Lambert typewriter as a subsidiary business. The typewriter failed as conspicuously as the gramophone succeeded; its sale was discontinued in 1904 and the company resumed its old name in 1908.

**46 Dog and trumpet
a) original form
with phonograph
b) final form with
gramophone**

a   b

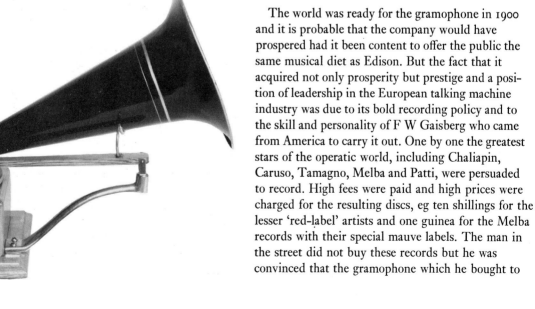

47 Hand-driven gramophone (Style No 2), 1898

48 The trade-mark model, 1898

46

The world was ready for the gramophone in 1900 and it is probable that the company would have prospered had it been content to offer the public the same musical diet as Edison. But the fact that it acquired not only prosperity but prestige and a position of leadership in the European talking machine industry was due to its bold recording policy and to the skill and personality of F W Gaisberg who came from America to carry it out. One by one the greatest stars of the operatic world, including Chaliapin, Caruso, Tamagno, Melba and Patti, were persuaded to record. High fees were paid and high prices were charged for the resulting discs, eg ten shillings for the lesser 'red-label' artists and one guinea for the Melba records with their special mauve labels. The man in the street did not buy these records but he was convinced that the gramophone which he bought to

The Gramophone Co.
I am very pleased with my latest records. Your wonderful
Gramophone improves year by year.

Nellie Melba

play his more popular records was a musical instrument and not a toy.

In 1900 seven different models of the gramophone were available in this country, called Styles No 2 to 7 and De Luxe. There was also a coin-slot model which was sold more successfully by the Berlin branch of the company than in England. Style No 2 was hand-driven and sold for £2 2s 0d. Style No 5 was the 'trade-mark' model at £5 10s 0d. The soundbox was an improvement on Berliner's, designed by Eldridge Johnson and by Alfred Clark, who was later to become chairman of the Gramophone Company. The Concert

soundbox was introduced in 1901 and the Exhibition model in 1903; this latter survived, with minor changes of design, until 1921. This group of instruments was rendered obsolescent by the introduction of 10″ discs in 1901 and obsolete by the 12″ discs of 1903. There followed a family of Monarch instruments comprising the Monarch (1901), Junior Monarch (1902), Senior Monarch (1905), Victor (1905, later Victor Monarch) and Intermediate Monarch (1908).

The most important technical development of the instrument came in 1903 when the tone arm was introduced. In earlier instruments the narrow end of

47

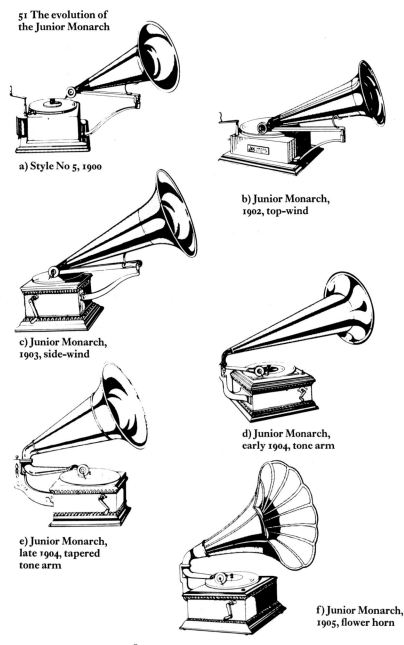

51 The evolution of the Junior Monarch

a) Style No 5, 1900

b) Junior Monarch, 1902, top-wind

c) Junior Monarch, 1903, side-wind

d) Junior Monarch, early 1904, tone arm

e) Junior Monarch, late 1904, tapered tone arm

f) Junior Monarch, 1905, flower horn

the horn was connected directly to the soundbox by a leather elbow and was carried across the record as the latter rotated. The introduction of the tone arm meant that the horn, now independent of the soundbox, could be left pointing in any desired direction and that the needle point pressure was reduced, as was also the mass to be set in motion by the groove wall. At first the tone arm was of uniform diameter but it was almost immediately tapered from horn to soundbox. It was this feature that the Victor Talking Machine Company in America and the Gramophone Company in Europe were able to defend successfully in the courts. Pathé instruments in France and Odeon and others in Germany were soon provided with tone arms, but they could not be tapered. The Pathé firm, losing a case on this issue in 1908, acknowledged defeat with good humour in the words 'New Pathé-phones, less tapered arms, give sweeter tones, and greater charms'. The tapered arm may well have given better reproduction than the non-tapered but the empirical methods of the times were well summed up in 1910 by the judge who, after listening patiently to expert evidence, said in his judgement–'I am not going into the theory of the amplification of sound, about which nobody seems to know anything whatever'.

The horn, having achieved independence, was now free to grow without the need for a supporting crane. The straight 'trumpet' which had given a somewhat ludicrous appearance to the early talking machines was now replaced by flower shaped horns pioneered by the Morning Glory, which was sold as an accessory in late 1904, appeared on the luxury Melba model of 1905 and was later supplied with all models. The exposed horn design reached its peak of elegance in the Sheraton model of 1906, which had a 12″ turntable and a speed indicator and was sold, mounted on a handsome pedestal, for £35. The drawing-room triumph of the flower horn was, however, short-lived.

far left
52 The Gramophone Company's first concealed horn model; the Gramophone Grand, 1907

left
53 The Gramophone Company's first 'hornless' model; the Pigmy Grand, 1909

below
54 The Gramophone Company's first table grand; Model 8, 1910

The same device that had enabled the horn to grow also enabled it to be concealed. In 1904 the Holzweissig firm in Leipzig had introduced an instrument called the Hymnophon, in which the horn was led through the case and only its bell protruded from the front. When this was advertised in England the selling point was the ease with which the instruments could be packed for transport but in the hands of the Victor Talking Machine Company concealment of the horn became the means whereby the gramophone could be not only tolerated but welcomed in the most exclusive drawing-room. The Gramophone Grand (Victor Victrola in America) of 1907, with a waist high cabinet in which the turntable was concealed by a lid and the horn beneath it by doors, achieved this object and also supplied, below the horn, a space for the storage

49

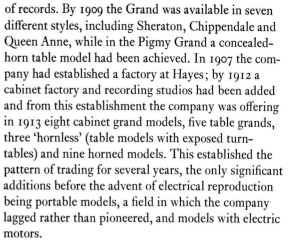

of records. By 1909 the Grand was available in seven different styles, including Sheraton, Chippendale and Queen Anne, while in the Pigmy Grand a concealed-horn table model had been achieved. In 1907 the company had established a factory at Hayes; by 1912 a cabinet factory and recording studios had been added and from this establishment the company was offering in 1913 eight cabinet grand models, five table grands, three 'hornless' (table models with exposed turntables) and nine horned models. This established the pattern of trading for several years, the only significant additions before the advent of electrical reproduction being portable models, a field in which the company lagged rather than pioneered, and models with electric motors.

55 (above)
The gramophone
entertained the
mighty

56 (below)
The phonograph
entertained the
humble and meek

THE PHONOGRAPH

50

After the Columbia Phonograph Company (General) moved its European headquarters to London in 1900 it began to manufacture moulded records called High Speed or Type XP. By 1903 thousands of records per month by British artists were being manufactured. After the introduction of the Disc Graphophone in 1902 there was no immediate reason for believing that the disc would eventually oust the cylinder, as can be seen from the fact that the record factory established at Wandsworth in 1905 was originally designed to turn out 10,000 cylinders and 5000 discs per day.

In 1905 there was introduced a cylinder of 6″ length, called the Premier, originally for use with a loud-speaking instrument, the Twentieth Century Graphophone. A slight increase in length of the standard cylinder, introduced in late 1906 on three English makes of record, namely Sterling, White and Edison Bell, produced no immediate response from Columbia, but a Blue Ribbon cylinder, of length 4½″, was manufactured in 1908 'to meet the demand for better class cylinders'. Columbia's response in America to the introduction of 4-minute Amberol cylinders by Edison in 1908 was to take over the sales of the plastic surfaced records of the Indestructible Record Company which introduced a 4-minute cylinder in 1909. When these appeared in England they were sold only by the factor Murdoch, who also supplied attachments for the conversion of certain Columbia instruments to play them. By 1912, when Edison introduced his indestructible cylinder, the Blue Amberol, Columbia had abandoned the moribund cylinder trade.

Between 1896 and 1910 at least 40 different models of Columbia cylinder instruments were manufactured in the United States, but the general line of stylistic and technical development can be followed by considering only instruments that were widely advertised in England and by ignoring coin-slot models, office dictation machines and special models designed to play both small and large diameter cylinders. Of the instruments imported in 1900, the cheap baseboard models, designed for the mass market, were the type Q and the Eagle (B). These and later models were widely imitated in France, Germany and Switzerland and some factors in England contrived to issue them under their own trade names (eg Dulcetto). In addition there were two models with the motor enclosed in a wooden cabinet, namely the Columbia (AT) for standard size records and the Grand (AG, HG and GG) for large-diameter records. The latter model was soon discontinued but the former evolved by successive changes of reproducer design into a group of models distinguished by a lyre-shaped reproducer called the Lyric, in which the stylus was held in contact with the record by means of a spring. The first of this group was the type AZ of 1904; the cheaper Jewel and Trump were introduced in 1906 and 1907 respectively, while the Sovereign, with a long mandrel to play the new 6″ length cylinders, appeared in 1905. Columbia broke right away from the Edison tradition with the introduction of cylinder machines with tone arms. The first of these to appear in England was the Crown of 1907, and it was followed in 1908 by the Coronet, which could play cylinders of 6″ length. Columbia's most original contribution to the development of the

57 Cylinder graphophones

a) Type Q, 1898

b) Type B (Eagle), 1897

c) Type AT; later version of model introduced in 1898

d) Type AZ with Lyric reproducer, 1905

e) Type BQ (Crown) with tone arm, 1907

58 Early disc graphophones

a) Type AJ, 1902 model

b) Type AJ, 1903 model

c) Type BD with tone arm, 1906

d) First concealed horn model; Symphony Grand, 1907

[53]

cylinder instrument, namely the friction amplifier, is mentioned in a later chapter.

While the technical and stylistic development of Columbia disc records and instruments was inevitably parallel to that of Victor, some of the company's attemps at innovation are not without interest. A 14″ disc, introduced in 1903, was short-lived. So also was Columbia's double-sided disc of 1904 which swiftly vanished (presumably as a result of a threat by the makers of Odeon records who held the relevant patents), to re-appear in late 1907. In this year Columbia also experimented with a disc having a laminated structure instead of the homogeneous composition then generally used. According to the company this was the result of its employment of Marconi as technical adviser. A flexible disc which made a brief appearance at this time was called the Marconi. The disc instruments sold in 1903 (AU, AK, AJ, AH, AY, AR in ascending order of price) showed no novel features; a 'string-pull' winding device introduced in 1904 did not find favour, and the only advantage claimed for the tone-arm instruments of 1905–1908 (eg Champion, Sterling, Majestic, Imperial, Regal, Regent, Prince) was the use of aluminium in the construction of the tone arms and the introduction on some models of a soundbox having a clip instead of a screw to hold the needle.

In its employment of the freedom of styling resulting from the introduction of the concealed horn Columbia at first took up a position intermediate between the restraint of the Victor and Gramophone Company designers and the extremism of certain European firms. While ready, and indeed anxious, to let a talking machine disguise its true function they were not prepared to go so far as to make it look like an airship. The first concealed horn model, the Symphony Grand of 1907, took the exterior form of an upright piano and in later catalogues certain talking machines masqueraded as Regency side tables and as executives' desks. In America these instruments were the harbingers of an era in which period styling ran riot and it was possible to pay over $1000 for a Columbia instrument, but wartime austerity prevented the perpetration of such excesses in Europe.

At the close of our period the activities of the European branch of the Columbia Phonograph Company (General) were directed by Louis (later Sir Louis) Sterling, who had come from the USA in 1903, at the age of twenty-four, to work for G & T Limited. For a year he managed the British Zonophone Company, then from 1905 to 1907 he ran the Russell Hunting Record Company, which manufactured Sterling cylinders. Following the failure of this firm he became managing director of a company that sold the Rena record and Rena machines (see p 30). When, late in 1909, the machine business of this firm was discontinued and its record business was taken over by Columbia, Sterling became the managing director of the British branch, and in 1914 he became European general manager, to inaugurate a period in which, as a result of his leadership, the company rose to a commanding position in the industry.

11
Edison Bell

below right
**61 Edison Bell Elf,
1907**

below
**60 Edison Bell's
British-made Gem,
1904**

In Chapter 6 we have traced the evolution of Edison Bell Consolidated Phonograph Company until 1903 when its Peckham factory was established. The period of prosperity during which the company had exploited its monopoly of the distribution of phonographs and graphophones was about to be interrupted by com-mercial competition and litigation with Edison's National Phonograph Company, now marketing its own products in England. The assault began in 1904 with an attempt through the courts to prevent the company from using the name Edison. But the original contract of 1892 had contained a clause that the name must appear on the distributed products, and the only consolation gained by the National Phonograph Company was the stipulation that the name was not to be used alone but only in association with the name Bell. The attack now took on a less ethical but more effective form; Edison Bell was informed that unless it abandoned the use of the name its supply of phonographs would be cut off. Edison Bell replied by turning some of its employees into fictitious Edison dealers through whom it obtained supplies. The National Phonograph Company then sued Edison Bell and

56

were successful on appeal (January 1908), while Edison Bell had the slight compensation of winning a libel action arising from a circular issued to dealers during the course of this struggle.

Meanwhile Edison Bell attempted to become independent of the supply of Edison instruments by increasing its production of the British-made versions of Edison's Gem and Standard instruments (introduced in 1904) and of their successors, the Elf, Imp, Era and Don (1907). But by now the increasing public preference for the disc instrument and the price war between cylinder manufacturers left little to be gained from the cylinder trade. Edison Bell therefore entered the disc business, although it persevered with the supply of cylinders until 1912. New process (NP) cylinders were introduced in 1908 and Edison's Amberol was countered in 1909 – rather belatedly owing to a factory fire – with a 4-minute record called the Crystol. Appropriate modifications were made to the Elf group of machines to enable them to play the new record.

When Edison Bell entered the disc field, the Gramophone Company and the other major recording companies were using 'needle-cut' recording while Pathé were using the 'phono-cut' (hill and dale). Edison Bell

62 Edison Bell A1 Discaphone, to play both needle-cut and phono-cut discs, 1908

63 J E Hough of Edison Bell

The constant litigation, the decline of the cylinder trade and the strain of the introduction of the new discs and instruments were too much for the finances of the company. Edisonia Ltd, which had been mortgaged, was put up for sale and bought by J E Hough himself who thereby gained control of the whole business. In reorganizing it he changed its name to J E Hough Ltd. At the same time he acquired the assets of a liquidated company which had produced Sterling cylinders and he continued for some time to sell records with this label. The smaller hill-and-dale disc survived for a year or two under the name Little Champion. The original needle-cut disc continued to sell at 2s 6d and acquired as its full title the Edison Bell Gramophone Record Bell Disc (the Gramophone Company having by now lost its exclusive right to the use of the word 'gramophone'). A superior one called the Velvet Face (10″ at 3s od and, later, 12″ at 4s od) made a modest assault on a better class market in 1911, while Hough's method of 'checkmating the German menace' was to introduce the Winner at 1s 6d, which started its long career in 1912.

If the name of Edison Bell rings loudly in the early history of the talking machine it is probably due more to the vigorous personality of J E Hough than to any technical developments initiated by the firm. Before he joined the company he fought stoutly against its monopoly and afterwards he fought equally stoutly in its defence. He engaged in the legal battle with the Edison interests with the same zest as in the commercial struggle against German manufacturers. As our period closed we find him making a characteristic contribution to the shooting war against the Germans by dismissing from his employment all men answering to the description of those required by Lord Kitchener for his new armies. Equally characteristic was his financial support of their families and his donation of thousands of records to the Forces.

used both. In July 1908 a 10½″ double-sided Bell Disc at 2s 6d was announced together with a pair of Phondiscs, one 12″ in diameter at 4s od and the other 8¾″ in diameter at 1s 6d (there is however no evidence that the 12″ Phondisc was ever made or sold). A group of Discaphone instruments, capable of playing both kinds of record, was also introduced.

"Humpty Dumpty had a great fall
"And all the κ cs - the Law's greatest men.
"Could'nt patch _ _ _ _ _ _ _ _ _ _ _ _ _

12

Unusual talking machines

Early talking machines were raucous but mercifully thin in tone. In 1897, however, Lioret demonstrated to the Société Française de Physique a most ingenious loudspeaking phonograph. The cylindrical record had

a celluloid surface and, in accordance with a process patented by Lioret in 1893, this surface was temporarily softened by means of hot water to receive the recorded impressions. These were of greater amplitude

65 Lioretgraph No 3, 1900

than could be achieved with wax, and the simple but effective reproducer devised by Lioret used a diaphragm of considerable diameter. His instrument was therefore audible in a large hall.

Lioret (1848–1938) had started his working life as a clockmaker but he entered the phonograph business in 1893 when commissioned by Émile Jumeau of Paris to provide a voice for one of his celebrated range of dolls. The idea was not new; hand-driven talking dolls had been produced in the USA by the Edison Toy Manufacturing Company from late 1887 to mid-1890, and in Germany Berliner's primitive gramophone mechanism had been fitted into a doll. But in his execution of the idea Lioret was a pioneer. He was

66 Advertisement for Lioret's salon and loud-speaking phonographs, 1897

61

67 Lioret talking doll, 1893

far right
68 Edison phonograph with duplex reproducer, 1896

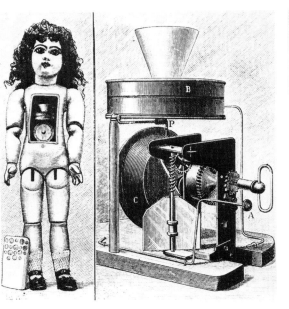

69 Columbia Multiplex Grand, 1900

among the first to drive a phonograph with a spring motor; he was the first to manufacture a moulded cylinder and he was the first to develop a cylinder of the type later known as 'indestructible'. His 4-minute record of 1898 was a decade ahead of Edison's Amberol. His under-capitalized firm could not compete with that associated with the brothers Pathé and he left the phonograph business in 1911, but he continued to be active in other fields of practical acoustics including sound films and (during and after the First World War) sound ranging and submarine detection.

The showman who wanted all the volume he could get had to use the biggest trumpet consistent with portability. Edison in 1896 produced a duplex reproducer whereby two such trumpets could be used and they could point in opposite directions when the exhibitor occupied the centre of the hall. This redistributed the sound without amplifying it, but in 1898 the Polyphone Company of Chicago marketed an attachment whereby a phonograph or graphophone could be provided with two soundboxes in tandem, each with its own horn. Hesitating purchasers were assured that this would not only provide more than double the normal volume but also produce 'the sweetness of many echoes instantly combined'. The multiplication of horns went a stage further when, at the Paris exhibition of 1900, Columbia showed their Multiplex Grand, having three horns and soundboxes in parallel. It was possible with this instrument to record the three parts of a trio on three separate sound tracks on the cylinder, in which case the reproduction would have stereophonic properties, but it is doubtful if this was the intention of the designer. Finally at the St Louis exhibition of 1904, Columbia produced a quadruple-disc Graphophone having four turntables mounted on a single vertical shaft, thus overtrumping Victor's Triplephone which entertained an audience of 20,000 at the Crystal Palace in the same year.

More sophisticated methods of increasing volume had by now been developed. One of these methods was to allow the vibrations of the reproducing stylus to modulate the flow of air passing from a compressor into the horn. The method had been envisaged by Edison in his British patent of 1878, and the principle had been successfully applied by the British engineer Short in 1898, but it was in the hands of Sir Charles Parsons, in 1902, that the technique was sufficiently perfected to become a commercial proposition. His 'Auxetophone' was demonstrated to the Royal Society in 1904, and the Gramophone Company began to market the instrument at £100 in 1906. Concerts were given with this machine in the Albert Hall and other concert halls; it was employed in public parks and at skating rinks, and a hornless version, in an elegant Chippendale cabinet, even invaded the drawing-room.

A rival to the Auxetophone, using a similar principle, was introduced by Pathé in 1907 under the name Orphone. Pathé also produced in 1909 another contribution to outdoor talking machine entertainment with their enormous 20″ disc played on an instrument called the Pathephone Majestic, with a turntable rotating at 120 rpm. An air-operated version of this instrument, installed in 1911 at a point on the route

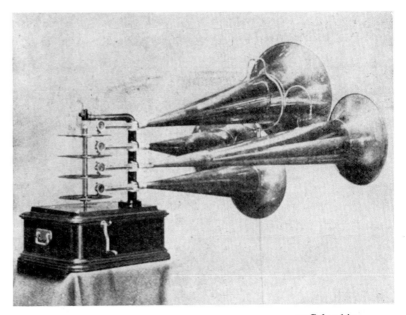

70 Columbia quadruple disc graphophone, 1904

71 Parsons Auxetophone attached to Gramophone Company instrument and standing on the compressor cabinet

63

of a state drive by King George V, made its contribution to the entente cordiale by blaring out the National Anthem when their Majesties appeared.

Both Auxetophone and Orphone found a ready market in Germany, where they were employed for restaurant entertainment. They were joined by another French instrument, the Gaumont Elgéphone, which had been announced as employing as its basic principle the modulation of a gas flame by the sound, but which, when it appeared, was found to employ the same principle as the other two instruments. German imita-

tions, adapted for coin-slot operation, quickly followed. Every possible form of motive power was employed to work the compressor including, as well as the hand pump and the electric motor, the falling weight, the water motor and the hot-air motor. Cylinders of carbon dioxide were also used, not without some misgivings being expressed as to the effect of this gas on the health and comfort of the unsuspecting audience. The volume produced by these instruments was still further increased by the use of Starkton discs, cut with a greater groove pitch than normal. In England

the Auxetophone met another rival in H A Gaydon's Stentorphone of 1910, which was employed not only in hotels and restaurants but also provided the sound for early talking films, and was used after the war as a somewhat inflexible public address system.

A third method of securing increased volume was introduced by Columbia on their Twentieth Century and Home Premier graphophones of 1905 and 1906 respectively. In these instruments the vibrations of the reproducer stylus were transmitted to a semi-circular friction shoe in rubbing contact with a rotat-ing pulley; the other end of this shoe was connected to the centre of a large diaphragm. The general prin-ciple had long been known and used in telephony, but its application to the talking machine was patented by Higham in 1901. These Columbia instruments per-formed excellently in the hands of experts but were too temperamental to gain general acceptance.

Increased volume was needed only for instruments used in the open air, in concert halls and in res-taurants, but the need for increased playing time for cylinders was more widely felt, especially after the

above left
74 Pathé compressed-air instrument, 1907

above
75 A German compressed-air instrument; Fortophon Starktonmaschine

advent of the 12″ disc. This requirement was eventually met in 1908 by Edison with his Amberols playing for 4 minutes; as a result of this development the 'Longest-Playing Phone', with a 16″ cylinder, offered in the same year, was still-born. An attempt to increase the playing time of the disc was made in 1912–1915 by the National Gramophone Company which marketed a fine-groove phono-cut disc called the Marathon, one of which achieved a playing time of 16½ minutes.

Attempts were made, both in England and Germany, to produce an instrument capable of playing both cylinders and discs, but neither the Twophone of 1903 nor the much more vigorously publicized Deuxphone of 1905 seems to have met with any commercial success. The spring-driven motor remained the only practical source of motive power for mass-produced

right
76 Gaydon Stentorphone, 1914

77 Columbia Home Premier loudspeaking graphophone, 1906

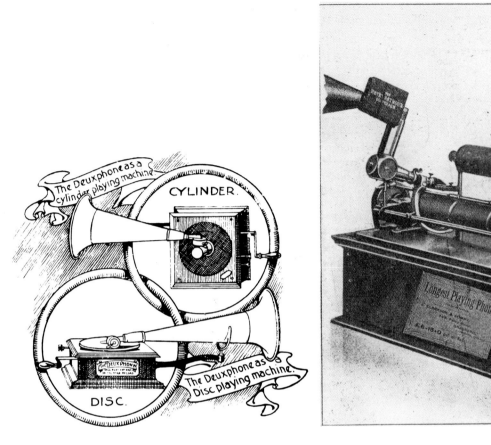

domestic instruments until the majority of house-holds were connected to the public electricity supply mains and even then the full advantages of electrical drive were realized only when these mains supplied alternating current. But one interesting experiment with motive power was made during this period, namely the use of a hot-air motor. An instrument with such a motor, made by the Swiss firm of Paillard, was shown at the spring Leipzig Fair of 1910 and it was later marketed in this country as the Apollo No 10. It ran for 12 hours with one charge of methylated

spirit. Of its claim to be both noiseless and fireproof only the former is consistent with the author's experience.

A curious instrument that appeared in 1908 was received with ridicule even by German dealers who were by then used to extravagancy of design. This was the Klingsor, which had a zither-like set of tuned metallic wires stretched across the mouth of the horn. The designer was somewhat vague in his claims regarding the precise function of these strings. Presumably, if they had any effect at all, they would reinforce

78 Longest playing phone with 16″ cylinder, 1908

left
79 Deuxphone, to play both cylinders and discs

67

**80 Apollo No 10,
driven by hot-air
motor, 1910**

**81 Klingsor talking
machine, 1908**

left
**82 Talking
clock, 1911**

below
**83 Stollwerck toy
talking machine
playing a chocolate
disc, 1903**

by resonance the discrete series of notes to which they were tuned, but an English advertiser asserted that 'the idea of the harp is to disseminate the sound in every direction of the room'. The patent specification envisaged the possibility of attaching a keyboard to the instrument and thereby providing a zither accompaniment to the record. Despite its cool reception, the instrument was commercially successful and it was marketed in this country, ultimately by Murdoch using locally made cabinets, until 1914 and beyond.

It is difficult for us to understand now the zeal with which early twentieth century inventors sought to substitute the imperfect utterances of the phonograph for the melodious chimes of bells or the evocative call of the cuckoo as a means of signalling the passage of time. Reports of the invention of a talking clock appeared frequently in the talking machine press but the least unsuccessful of these efforts seems to have been that of A Newman of Berlin. His 1911 instrument was remarkable in that the time announcements were recorded as 48 tracks on a perforated celluloid film, one for each quarter hour of twelve hours. In his 1914 instrument, however, Hiller reverted to the disc.

The Stollwerck gramophone of 1903, playing a

chocolate record which could ultimately be eaten by the purchaser, was clearly not meant to be taken seriously. But considerable interest was aroused by an announcement in the *Phonographische Zeitschrift* that a French firm was about to introduce a disc of about 3″ diameter which was to play for 5 minutes using a hardened bee-sting as a reproducing stylus. However the name of the inventor was given as Humeur Davrille and the announcement appeared on 1 April (1910). It was possibly a satirical allusion by the editor to the many preposterous projects that wasted the time of the Patent Office staffs during a period in which the development of the talking machine was unaccompanied by any scientific investigation of the basic principles. The seed of such a disciplined study was sown in 1920 when Guest and Merriman recorded electrically parts of the burial service of the unknown warrior in Westminster Abbey. But our period closes in 1914 when the progress in Europe of the 'industry of human happiness' which Edison had founded was temporarily checked and many of its factories were converted for the production of human misery instead.

right
84 Guard mounting to gramophone music

far right
85 'It's your duty, lad', 1914

Further Reading

For the general reader

Roland Gelatt. *The Fabulous Phonograph* (*2nd Edition 1977*). A highly entertaining yet accurate account of the history of an invention, an industry and a musical instrument, with the latter aspect stressed.

Oliver Read and Walter L Welch. *From Tin Foil to Stereo* (*2nd Edition 1976*). A comprehensive account with an emphasis on the technical and commercial history of sound recording and with a wealth of illustration. An extensive bibliography is provided.

For the instrument collector

Christopher Proudfoot. *Collecting Phonographs and Gramophones* (*1980*). A well illustrated book, with many of the pictures in colour, which concentrates on the instruments that collectors are likely to meet with, and gives advice on acquisition and repair.

Howard Hazelcorn. *A Collector's Guide to the Columbia Spring-wound Cylinder Graphophone 1894–1910* (*1976*). A booklet that has made possible for the first time the precise identification and dating of Columbia cylinder instruments.

George L Frow and Albert F Sefl. *The Edison Cylinder Phonographs 1877–1929* (*1978*). A work whose comprehensiveness, accuracy and scholarship have set new standards in this field of study. Contains an extensive bibliography.

E Bayly. *The EMI Collection* (*2nd Edition 1977*). Nearly three hundred instruments are illustrated and described, some fifty being of Berliner or HMV origin and the remainder mostly from continental Europe.

Periodicals

The Hillandale News, organ of the City of London Phonograph and Gramophone Society (bi-monthly since October 1960).

The Talking Machine Review International (bi-monthly since December 1969).

The back numbers of both these periodicals contain a wealth of historical information on phonographs, gramophones, cylinders, discs, recording artists, firms, personalities in the recording industry etc, together with hints on the acquisition, care and maintenance of talking machines. In addition articles appearing in these periodicals, and discographies encouraged by their editors are gradually unfolding the full story of the 78 rpm gramophone record in the UK.

The Antique Phonograph Monthly (ten issues annually since 1973). The periodical serves specifically the interests of American collectors, but most issues contain articles of value to all who are interested in the history of the talking machine.

Exhibition Catalogues

The centenary of the invention of reproduced sound (1977) was commemorated by a number of exhibitions whose catalogues have more than ephemeral value. They include:

A Wonderful Invention. An exhibition at the Library of Congress, Washington. Catalogue edited by Iris Bodin and Randall S Koladis. Introduction by James R Smart and Jon W Newsam.

100 Years of Recorded Sound. An exhibition by the City of London Phonograph and Gramophone Society and the British Institute of Recorded Sound. Compiled by Christopher Proudfoot, assisted by Frank Andrews.

Le Magasin du Phonographe. An exhibition organized in Brussels by the Credit Communal de Belgique. Compiled by Gérard Valet.

Phonographs and Gramophones. An exhibition at the Royal Scottish Museum Edinburgh. Compiled by Alistair G Thomson.

The first two of these catalogues have instructive introductions. The introduction to the third is meant to entertain rather than to instruct.

For the historian

Peter Ford. Mr Ford surveyed the technical history of sound recording in a series of 5 articles in *Recorded Sound* (Nos 7, 8, 9, 10–11 and 13) and in a series of 36 articles in Hi-Fi News from January 1960 to July 1963. Although the centenary of reproduced sound

(1977) produced a number of historical surveys, these articles still remain the best source for the technical history of sound recording in the period covered by this booklet.

Warren Rex Isom. The most comprehensive of the 1977 surveys was the centennial issue (Oct-Nov 1977) of the *Journal of the Audio Engineering Society*, edited by Warren Rex Isom, in which 33 authors were invited to include a mention of the past, to emphasize the present and to guess what the future might be. Some of the authors did rather more than glance at the past so that the resulting volume has much historical interest.

Symposium. In July 1977 a symposium was held at the Royal Scottish Museum Edinburgh to commemorate the centenary of reproduced sound. The published proceedings, entitled *Phonographs and Gramophones*, contain several articles revealing the results of recent painstaking research into various historical aspects of sound recording and reproduction. The topics range from a re-examination of the circumstances of the invention of the tinfoil phonograph to a study of the evolution of the gramophone as an article of furniture.

Discography

Discographers have been very active in the decade since this booklet was first published and the exacting standards now set can be achieved only by the most dedicated practitioners of the art. Discography is, however, outside the scope of this booklet but one example should be mentioned, since the volume concerned contains not only a comprehensive study of

the Edison cylinder record but also an excellent intro-
ductory chapter on the early history of the phonograph. This volume is Allen Koenigsberg's *Edison
Cylinder Records (1899–1912)*, published in 1969.

From France and Germany

Paul Charbon. The talking machine in France has
found its historian in M Charbon. So far he has
written at length on the story of magnetic recording
(*Diapason*, from May 1972 to April 1974) and he has
initiated a series of articles on French phonograph
pioneers including Scott de Martinville, Cros, Lioret
and Pathé (*Hi-Fi Stereo* March 1978 and later issues).
He contributed to the commemoration of the
centenary of reproduced sound (1977) with the lavishly
illustrated book *Le Phonographe à la Belle Époque*, and
his most recent (1981) volume, *La Machine Paylante*,
deals generally with the invention and early

development of the talking machine, and particularly
with the work of the French pioneers.

Herbert Jüttemann. *Phonographen und Gramophone*
(1979). The author surveys the history of the
gramophone up to 1930, emphasizing the technical
rather than the commercial aspect and mentioning,
but not concentrating on, German contributions.
An unusual feature of the book is a series of chapters
dealing separately with the development of machines
in general, motors, soundboxes, horns and records.

Walter Bruch. The distinguished inventor of the
PAL system of colour television gave a survey of
gramophone history up to 1960 in a series of articles
in *Funkschau* (between December 1977 and April
1979), dealing authoritatively with technical
developments especially in the latter part of his
period.

Indexes

Index of Persons